# CAREER Wise

## PROVEN STRATEGIES FOR THRIVING AT WORK

**Danella Schiffer, Ph.D.**

**Author's Note:**

While examples and case studies presented in this book are real, the names and identifying characteristics of companies and individuals have been altered to protect their confidentiality. As such, any resemblance to a specific individual or company is coincidental.

The ideas and advice contained in this book may not apply to every individual and situation. You should consult with a professional where appropriate. The author shall not be liable for any loss or damage allegedly arising from any information or advice contained in this book.

**Published by Danella Schiffer**
danella.schiffer@att.net

Cover and interior design: Gary A. Rosenberg
Produced by The Book Couple • www.thebookcouple.com

# Contents

# Acknowledgments

This book could not have been written without the willingness of my clients to open up and allow me to learn what makes them tick. I am also indebted to the corporate staff who made my work possible. Special thanks go to Victor Viggiano, Bernard Cammarata, Sylvia Wagner, Bruce Margolis, and my former mentor, Jerry Beam. My mother, Justine, deserves abundant thanks for her support and encouragement over the years. My deepest gratitude goes to Stacie Weiner, who edited the early manuscript, thereby helping to ensure that it was not overly academic or inappropriately irreverent.

With the expert help of Carol and Gary Rosenberg of The Book Couple, the manuscript became a book.

Final thanks go to the success stories and screwups that we read about on a regular basis, thereby providing a rich source for learning about effective career management.

# Introduction

We've all witnessed presumably smart and capable people derail their careers. This occurs in all professions and places of work. Most often, the self-destruction is subtle and occurs over time. At times though, it is flagrant and newsworthy—as with a venerable politician who becomes the center of a sex scandal. Clearly, valuable lessons can be learned from observing why some fail and, conversely, what contributes to success.

As an industrial/organizational psychologist who has worked in diverse settings over thirty years, I have had the opportunity to witness, firsthand, downfalls and success stories. Two key components of my work have served as an observation deck. The first is the career assessment. Over the years I have assessed hundreds of people at varying levels, all the way up to chief executive officer. Why would an organization want to assess an individual? The purpose of an assessment is to help management make more informed career management decisions, whether the decision involves hiring, promoting, or reassigning someone.

Every assessment looks at three broad categories of personal functioning:

- How does an individual think, solve problems, and make decisions?

- What is an individual's personality? How does a person relate to others?

- What motivates someone to work hard and do his or her best?

In a nutshell, the assessment tries to answer these questions: What is this person all about? What are the person's assets and potential liabilities? What does the individual need to do in order to thrive in his or her career?

The assessment is also the foundation for business coaching, which is another component of my work. As a business coach, I work with people who need to modify counterproductive behaviors or develop new skills to function more effectively. Many have high potential but can benefit from some "tweaking." Others are in danger of derailing their careers.

With a wealth of information gleaned from those with whom I have worked, two skill areas in particular stand out as being directly related to surviving and ultimately thriving in one's career:

1. **the ability to think rationally** and

2. **the ability to relate effectively.**

In light of these two key skill areas, one could then ask the question, "So why do smart people do dumb things?" and, in a similar vein, "Why do nice people flounder in their relationships?" Hopefully, you'll be able to answer these questions after reading this book. By applying the proven strategies that follow, careers can take off.

## What You Will Find in This Book

**Chapter 1** provides a tongue-in-cheek look at what can happen when an individual has serious limitations in his or her ability to think, relate, or both. Lacking in common sense, basic social skills, and interpersonal savvy will almost certainly block career progress.

**Chapter 2** directs the reader inwardly. Basic to any successful career is first ensuring that the right career path has been chosen. Strong self-esteem is another fundamental component. Rarely are self-doubters able to rise to their potential. Next, we talk about emotional intelligence, which is the foundation for managing relationships.

**Chapter 3** focuses on strategies for building strong relationships. By understanding the *feel good factor* and the importance of pressing *warm buttons,* you will be poised to get people on your side, which equates to building a constituency. Finally, there is a discussion of *influencing,* which represents relationship management at perhaps its highest level. Only individuals with strong people savvy can persuade others, without having authority over them, to do what they want others to do.

**Chapter 4** builds on the preceding concepts and focuses on managing the boss. As stated in the opening paragraph, "Being a star performer does not guarantee career success. Often, it is how well you manage the relationship with your boss that can make or break your future in a company."

**Chapter 5** addresses *healthy confrontation.* By the time you read about the *four simple words* to avoid an unnecessary confrontation, you will realize just how important it is to be strong in the art of relationship management.

**Chapter 6** shifts the focus from being people smart to thinking smartly. We begin with an overview of basic principles that guide sound thinking. Next is a discussion of *thinking traps* that can derail sound thinking. A discussion of *critical thinking* follows, which describes the kind of thought necessary for making important decisions. Finally, we look at the appropriateness of changing one's mind: Weakness or strength? That is the question.

**Chapter 7** deals with an inevitable aspect of work: stress. The first two sections take a rational approach to stress management. Here, you'll learn how to *think* your way through stress—that is, methodically assess a problem and develop strategies for dealing with it. While physical approaches such as deep breathing and muscle relaxation allow one to chill out and refresh, neither addresses the causal problem.

The third section reviews typical *bumps in the road* that you may encounter during your career. Whether they involve getting a new boss, a cut in compensation, or denial of a promised promotion, each is stressful and requires rational thinking, social judgment, and the ability to confront productively—all skills you will have learned about in previous sections.

**Chapter 8** takes a look at the subject of image management—that is, the art of projecting oneself in a favorable light. You'll learn about *good, bad,* and *ugly* image management and hopefully settle on the first. Tips for managing your image effectively are offered.

**Chapter 9** concludes with a look at career growth when moving up the traditional ladder is not available. Here, you'll learn how to assess if moving up to a higher level is right for you. If not, some ideas for how to grow in place are offered.

Each chapter is intended to help you to more skill-fully navigate your career in today's competitive and tight job market, reach your potential, and enjoy greater satisfaction. The skills presented also have broad applicability to our everyday lives.

# CHAPTER 1

❖❖❖

# *Why You Need to Read On*

## How to Shoot Yourself in the Foot During a Job Interview

By the time an individual meets with me for a prehire assessment, the candidate has been carefully screened by the company. Most applicants are highly qualified, and my job is to determine who represents a good fit with the company.

It is self-evident that job candidates strive to be on their best behavior during an interview. It is therefore important to seriously consider startling behavior that suggests a questionable hiring choice. Based on my most memorable assessments, the following are some of the things candidates can do to shoot themselves in the foot.

1. **Demonstrate good personal hygiene.** A candidate for the presidency of a retail company came to the assessment with his breakfast in hand: a container of coffee and a muffin. He asked, apologetically, if it

would be okay to eat during the session, explaining that he had been caught in traffic and had not had time to eat beforehand. After finishing his food, he reached into his shirt pocket, pulled out dental floss, and proceeded to clean his teeth. To his credit, he continued to respond to questions while flossing, demonstrating an excellent ability to multitask.

2. **Make the most of your interview visit.** A chief marketing officer candidate made a favorable impression during his interview. After that, he was given written tests to be completed in the conference room, with a break for lunch. Surprised to learn that he had not completed the tests, I checked with the hotel's concierge to inquire further and was told that the candidate had returned to his room with a young lady and had left the inn several hours later. The candidate sent an e-mail the next day to say that he was unable to finish in time and would put the remainder of the tests in the mail. Trying not to jump to conclusions, I briefly considered the possibility that the candidate's behavior represented team-oriented problem solving.

3. **Be clever. Share your knowledge of the animal kingdom.** A candidate for manager of store operations presented a sullen demeanor, until I asked him to identify an animal that he might like to be if not himself. His face lit up as he responded, "I definitely

would be a lurkfish." He explained his choice by noting that the lurkfish is patient and resourceful. Curious, I researched the animal afterward and learned the following: *The lurkfish is camouflaged to hide from enemies and ambush prey. Lying in the shallows of a swamp, sometimes for days on end, the lurkfish waits for a victim to pass. It then uses its powerful tail to dart forward and snap up its prey.* On the positive side, one might infer that the candidate has disciplined eating habits.

4. **Take charge and make your presence felt in a big way.** An imposing candidate for chief operating officer greeted me with, "Just to make things clear, I view this as intrusive and will not respond to questions that I don't like." His take-charge and abrasive style was evident throughout the interview. He was particularly proud of his independent streak, stating that it had emerged during childhood and could be seen in his getting A's in all academic subjects and a D in conduct. He was never at a loss for words, except when asked how he builds morale and makes colleagues "feel good."

5. **Be yourself. Demonstrate candor.** During the assessment, candidates are asked to create stories from pictures on cards. One depicts a man on a rope. Frequently, a story is told about someone climbing or descending the rope in a competition. In one case, a

gregarious sales candidate responded instantaneously as follows: "A naked gentleman is climbing down a rope, trying to escape his girlfriend's bedroom after hearing her husband come home unexpectedly." Encouraged by my accepting nod, the remainder of the interview proved to be similarly entertaining.

Try testing your diagnostic skills by matching the following hiring risks to each candidate just described. One or more characteristics may apply to each person.

## Potential Hiring Risks

a. Difficulty in the interpersonal arena; potential to alienate colleagues

b. Poor impulse control; unable to filter remarks

c. Poor social judgment

d. Questionable reliability and work ethic

e. Operates according to own agenda

f. Questionable common sense

# CHAPTER 2

◈

# *Looking Inwardly*

## Moving Toward the Right Career Path

Some of you may be out of work or looking for your first job. Others may be underemployed or just unhappy with your job situation. Some may be ready to take a different path. So where do you begin to launch or rekindle your career? A good place to start is to look inwardly and better understand yourself relative to your career goals. Only then can you identify a path that represents a "good fit."

As an industrial/organizational psychologist, I am often called upon to evaluate candidates for jobs. The primary goal of every evaluation is to answer these questions: "Is there a good fit between the candidate, the job, and the company?" and "Does the individual have the right mix of abilities, personality attributes, and motivation to succeed?" Experience suggests that three broad categories of individual functioning best answer the "good fit" questions: (1) intelligence and thinking/work style, (2) personality traits and how one relates to others, and (3) motivational needs and interests. Let's look at examples within each category:

- **Intelligence and thinking/work style.** The way you think and approach tasks is an important consideration. Do you welcome complex challenges and new learning? Are you a creative problem solver, or do you prefer tried and true solutions? Do you like to work on one thing at a time or multitask? Do you prefer to plan or execute? Do you focus more on details or the big picture? Are you methodical or unstructured in getting things done?

- **Personality traits and how you relate to others.** One's personality is made up of many facets. Do you prefer working with a lot of personal space or do you thrive when working closely with others? Are you warm and gregarious or reserved and quiet? Do you like to be in charge or are you accommodating and comfortable taking a back seat? Patient or impatient? Sensitive or thick skinned? Laid back or intense?

- **Motivational needs and interests.** Here, we are concerned with what we enjoy doing most and what drives us to work hard at something. Is it money, power, fame, or a need to contribute to others' welfare? Or is it a need to achieve a high level of competency in some area? On the other hand, some people have limited ambition. They may be more motivated, for example, to focus energy on their families. This is not a value judgment, but it is important to know.

A few examples will shed light on making career choices. During an appointment with an endodontist for root canal treatment, I asked why he chose that particular career path. He indicated that he originally chose dentistry to follow in his father's footsteps. However, needing predictability in his life, he wanted to specialize in an area that involved more sameness than variability in his daily schedule. He also wanted a career that required a high level of skill but not constant new learning. Given his abilities, temperament, and interests, endodontics turned out to be a good fit.

A manufacturing company that was downsizing its workforce asked me to counsel a group of terminated engineers. One in particular stood out. He was a reserved and kindhearted man who was bent on buying a business rather than joining another company. While his wife urged him to buy a fast-food franchise, he was not convinced. After conducting a career assessment, it became clear that business ownership was appropriate and that the service industry would be a good fit, given the pleasure he derived from helping people. When he cancelled one of our appointments to attend a funeral, I thought, "Eureka!"—with his somber demeanor and compassionate nature, he had the right mix of qualities to succeed in the funeral business. He took that route and found satisfaction as a funeral director.

While obtaining professional guidance to find the right career path can be helpful, you can learn a lot about yourself on your own. Think about yourself relative to the three "good fit" categories and compare your self-perception with how others see you. Feel free to add traits that you consider relevant. Reflect on your experiences—that is, what you enjoy and dislike doing, the successes and mistakes you have experienced. Ideally, find a career path that drives your passion. Then work becomes pleasure.

## Self-Esteem and Career Success

With positive self-esteem being so important to career success, few could rise to their potential without it. By definition, self-esteem concerns how we view ourselves. When positive, one can look in the mirror and see someone who is valued and appreciated, capable and accomplished in some area, and in control of his or her life. At work, such people typically project confidence, are able to overcome adversity, make things happen, and cope effectively with stress. They also tend to adapt more easily to change, display initiative, and take risks. Those with a poor self-image might be reluctant to take on difficult challenges, try again after failing, or stand up for their beliefs. Nonetheless, some insecure people manage to rise to prominent positions. Fortunately, or unfortunately as the case may be, many end up self-destructing.

Poor self-esteem can be disguised in numerous forms. I recently coached a marketing executive whose career was stagnant because of his tendency to personalize criticism and respond angrily when his expertise was questioned. As it turned out, this individual experienced wavering self-esteem that was exacerbated by what he perceived to be rejection of his expertise. With coaching, he overcame his insecurity and recognized that colleagues often had their own agendas. As such, they did not necessarily reject his ideas on the basis of merit. In another instance, the president of a software company was known for his aggressive and intimidating manner, which had led to high turnover. Underneath his confident façade was a man with surprisingly poor self-esteem who used intimidation to ward off challenges from staff. He eventually learned to relate more effectively and voluntarily renamed his private plane from *Genghis Khan,* his former role model, to another name.

Inevitably, there are times when we experience self-doubt at work or in our personal lives. Triggers can include job loss, failure, disappointment, rejection by a loved one, or feeling unappreciated, to name a few. So how can our self-esteem survive such assaults? With profound wisdom, Eleanor Roosevelt once remarked, "No one can make you feel inferior without your consent."

In other words, you can choose to feel good about yourself, even when your self-esteem is tested. The following strategies can also help:

- **Choose companionship carefully.** When possible, surround yourself with people who make you feel good, avoiding those who drag you down.

- **Pursue activities that showcase your abilities.** If you are a skilled woodworker, embark on a project that leads to a tangible accomplishment.

- **Take charge of your life rather than allow things to "happen to you."** Become more comfortable saying "No" when you feel imposed upon. In a job search, actively network to get the leads needed to eventually land a job.

- **Get in the habit of practicing self-affirmation.** Focus on your attributes.

We also need to consider the impact of our words and behavior on others' self-esteem. Whether acting as a boss, parent, or someone engaging the services of another, consider the following:

- **Focus criticism on the issue and not the person.** Hence, if a painter misses a spot, point to the error rather than refer to his or her "sloppy" work.

- **Balance criticism with praise and encouragement.** Express your delight in another's accomplishment.

- Set realistic goals and expectations so that achievement is possible.

- **Empower others to do their jobs without overcontrolling them.** This conveys trust and allows people the space to flourish.

## Emotional Intelligence at Work

Why is it that some people with superior intellectual capacity are unable to get far in their careers while those less endowed manage to succeed? One reason worth examining concerns a different way of being smart other than having a high IQ.

Research over the past twenty years suggests that *emotional intelligence,* referred to as EQ (the *Q* stands for "quotient"), is a significant contributor to success in the business world. Simply put, EQ refers to *one's ability to perceive emotions, read interpersonal cues, and tune into others' needs and feelings in order to relate appropriately and get people to do what one wants them to do.*

I once evaluated a morale problem in a manufacturing company whose plant manager had a reputation for being brilliant but callous. Insisting that he was tough-minded but caring, I interviewed those who reported directly to him to learn how he was perceived by staff. One incident described to me was especially telling. Jane, a direct report, had just returned from vacation with a cast on her arm—the result of a fall. During a team meeting, Jane requested to leave early for a medical appointment. The boss, never acknowledging her obvious accident, ignored the request and instead indicated that she needed to work overtime to meet a new deadline. The team was aghast at his insensitivity and noted confidentially that they would do the bare minimum to keep their jobs. In the end, it was the boss's limited emotional intelligence that undermined morale and threatened productivity.

Experts view emotional intelligence as a progression of emotional learning, analyzed as follows:[1]

- **Identification of one's own emotions.** This is the foundation for emotional intelligence and represents self-awareness. Do you recognize when you are angry, frustrated, or joyful? Do you deny having feelings or place little importance on them?

- **Managing emotions.** How well do you handle your emotions? Can you bounce back from disappointment? Can you control your temper? Workplace rampages are a prime example of mismanaged emotions, emanating from uncontrollable rage.

- **Motivating oneself.** With emotions under control, one is able to focus energy on a goal through self-discipline, enthusiasm, and optimism.

---

1. P. Salovey and J. D. Mayer. (1990). Emotional intelligence. *Imagination, Cognition, and Personality, 9,* 185–211.

- **Recognizing others' emotions.** Empathy is a crucial social skill. Are you able to recognize others' emotions and "feel" with them? Can you "read" people—that is, understand where they are coming from?

- **Handling relationships.** The pinnacle of emotional intelligence is the ability to manage emotions in others. Can you calm down an angry customer? Can you rev up and motivate discouraged staff? Are you able to influence decision making?

The application of emotional intelligence is referred to as *emotional competence,* which is critical for career paths that involve working closely with people. Let's look at sales. It is human nature to buy a product from someone you like and trust. This notion is supported by research conducted in a national insurance company where it was concluded that sales agents with greater emotional competencies sold significantly more policies. In another study involving physicians, it was found that those with the best bedside manner—that is, those who were liked by their patients—had the fewest malpractice lawsuits, even though they may have been at fault. Those in management positions clearly benefit from having emotional competencies that enable them to lead effectively.

While emotional intelligence is typically developed during childhood, you can improve at any point in life. As a start, try the following steps:

- **Become more introspective.** Think about how you feel at any given moment and define your emotions.

- **Recognize when emotions are about to get the best of you and practice self-control.** For example, take a deep breath to calm down, or walk away.

- **When interacting, focus on the person, not just the words or issue.** Identify the person's thoughts, feelings, and motivations.

- **After an encounter with someone, think about how you came across.** What was your impact on the person? How did you make him or her feel?

- **Identify a role model who exemplifies emotional competence.** Observe the person carefully, noting specific behaviors that make him or her effective in relating to others. Why do you like being around the person?

# CHAPTER 3

# Relating Effectively

## Managing Relationships:
## The Pinnacle of Emotional Intelligence

It takes a high level of emotional intelligence to effectively manage relationships. Getting along well with others is just the first step. How many people do we know who are friendly and accommodating, who easily make friends at work but who cannot get co-workers to help out when they are behind schedule? Or perhaps they have sound ideas but cannot convince others to try them out. Getting people to do what you want them to do—the ability to influence or persuade without direct authority—is relationship management at its best.

A textbook case that vividly comes to mind involved a newly hired senior marketing executive who was very knowledgeable and experienced. The hiring assessment revealed numerous strengths but also uncovered qualities that could undermine his ability to build strong relationships. He was hired nevertheless. With broad-based experience, colleagues trusted his knowledge of marketing. He was also pleasant and team spirited. Within a year, however, it became apparent that he could not connect on a personal level. Being enigmatic and difficult to read, colleagues were never quite certain where he was coming from, which in turn led to distrust. In the end, he was unable to get colleagues on board with his recommendations for marketing initiatives. Coaching was not an option since he was not introspective or able to take a hard look at himself. Dismissing feedback from senior management and blaming the organization for his failure to relate effectively, he was encouraged to resign with a termination package.

In the following paragraphs and in the series of sections after that, we'll explore more fully what helps and hinders the building of strong relationships.

**The credibility factor.** The foundation of effective relationship management is the ability to earn credibility—that is, trustworthiness. Unless one is believable, respect is hard to earn. In "Coping with a Difficult Boss (Part 1)" in Chapter 4, I describe a newly hired senior executive who, by failing to add value to his team, was unable to earn credibility. As such, his ability to lead was greatly impaired. But credibility is more than just possessing subject-matter expertise. The marketing executive's credibility was undermined by his enigmatic qualities. Unable to "read" him, colleagues could not trust him.

**Let others know where you are coming from.** Picking up on the last point, recall a time when you were unable to "read" someone. Perhaps he or she smiled all the time, even when delivering serious news; or never shared deep feelings, relating only on a surface level; or worse, in an attempt to come across as thick-skinned, projected callousness instead. Consider the following example: The branch manager of a regional bank had difficulty connecting with people and a reputation for being coldhearted. He was offered coaching. During an early coaching session, he mentioned that his canine companion of fifteen years had died the previous weekend. After I offered words of support, he retorted matter-of-factly, "I'm okay with it. Pets don't live forever." However, he eventually revealed how lonely he felt. Others will tell you what they think you want to hear, or they will relate half-truths so that you never hear the whole story from them. In each case, by suppressing real feelings or holding back information, you cannot relate in an open and honest way, which is a prerequisite for building strong relationships.

**Keep your self-interest to yourself.** It is natural for individuals to look out for themselves. Nevertheless, once someone is perceived as operating according to his or her own agenda, resentment builds and trust erodes.

Several years ago, a client company described the derailment of a fast-track manufacturing executive. He apparently "wore his ambitions on his sleeve," boasting at every opportunity about how he would become the youngest group president in the company's history. His peer group soon learned to distrust his motives and then resisted supporting his ideas. Unable to work effectively in a team environment, his upward career trajectory came to a halt.

**Leave territorialism to the animal kingdom.** The image of executives prowling around the office and spraying their boundaries to keep out the competition is all too familiar. The problem is that the so-called competition is their peer group. It is fair to say that the most common form of group conflict stems from territorialism. For example, two merchandise executives in a retail company were embroiled in a battle over who legitimately was responsible for a particular accessory product, with each claiming that the other had no right to do business with the vendor. The conflict spilled over to staff and eventually caught the vendor in the middle. Intergroup relationships were strained and ultimately, the company's ability to negotiate the best deals with the vendor was impaired. With an intervention to resolve the conflict, the two executives, who never liked each other from the start (and probably never will), realized that in the best interest of the company they needed to resolve their differences and work as a team.

## The Feel Good Factor

Many years ago while working for an outplacement firm, I discovered a valuable principle that has stayed with me. Simply put, when in a negative place in your life, such as being unemployed, it's important to stay positive. One way is to surround yourself with people who make you *feel good*. Perhaps you have a friend who values your judgment and asks for your advice, or a distant relative remembers you on important holidays. This principle has particular relevancy in the work environment. In "Managing Up: You and the Boss" in Chapter 4, the importance of making your boss *feel good* in addition to helping him or her to look good is discussed. Expanding the *feel good* factor more broadly: People will gravitate to you if they *feel good* in your presence.

Think about people who make you *feel good*. What do they do or say?

**Connecting through empathy.** Empathy is a crucial social skill that enables people to convey caring. It is a two-step process. The first is to be able to read people and understand their feelings. The second is to feel with them and, importantly, make it known that you are attuned to their feelings. A salesman loses a large sale to a competitor. A colleague, sensing his disappointment tells him, "It must be discouraging to have put so much effort into the sale and lose it." The branch manager who could not reveal his sense of loneliness upon losing his beloved dog is unlikely to show empathy toward others who experience a similar loss. In the opposite vein, one can empathize with another's joy. A co-worker arrives at work beaming with pride and mentions that his son just received an athletic scholarship. Empathically you respond, "It must feel great to be the parent of such a talented young man."

Often I am asked the question, "Can I make tough people decisions and show empathy at the same time?" The answer is a resounding "Yes." Let's say that a boss has decided to withhold a bonus to a much-liked staff member who has underperformed. The staff member expresses his disappointment to his boss through a downtrodden expression. An empathic boss can respond by saying, "I understand your disappointment and will work closely with you to help you get a bonus the next time around."

**Awareness of one's impact on others.** Relating to people in a sensitive manner requires you to have an awareness of how you come across. I recently coached a hard-driving manager who genuinely cared about her staff. Nevertheless, she had a reputation for being blunt to the point of showing insensitivity. Her intention was to deal with staff in a forthright manner and quickly get to the point. But in so doing, she neglected to consider how different staff might interpret her words. Those who were experienced and confident were okay with her style, while others felt intimidated.

People who are most skilled in the interpersonal arena pay close attention to others' reactions and ask themselves, "How am I coming across?" Only then can they respond appropriately and connect in a meaningful way.

**Act as if you like someone.** There is no better way to win others over than by showing appreciation. There are numerous ways to do this:

- *Offer deserved praise.* This action is high on the list. It is not uncommon for managers to freely provide constructive criticism and be stingy with praise. The same goes in general for friends, parents, and loved ones. Striking a balance between the two will go a long way toward building strong relationships.

- *Let others know when they do something you admire.* For example, a manager might e-mail a staff member to praise her skillful handling of a difficult question at a meeting.

- *Make a thoughtful gesture.* I vividly remember coaching a woman who brought me a cup of my favorite coffee every time we met. This was indeed a thoughtful gesture and made me *feel good.*

- *Demonstrate loyalty whenever you can.* Coming to the defense of a colleague who is unjustly criticized is one way. Or helping a friend network for a better career opportunity is another. These are just two examples of showing your loyalty.

Artful relationship management can make or break a career. One memorable assignment of mine was the evaluation of a senior-level executive for the presidency of a company. His track record was impressive, having taken a fledgling organization and making it highly profitable. So how did he do it? Upon meeting him, I was struck by his gracious demeanor and ability to relate genuinely. The assessment further pointed to an inspirational leader who worked well through staff, bringing out the best in each. It was therefore not unexpected when he modestly indicated that the best ideas came from staff. Surprisingly, his intelligence tested only within the average range, which is significantly lower than typical for a senior-level executive. One could legitimately conclude that the candidate compensated for intellectual limitations with outstanding relationship-management and leadership skills. Making people *feel good* and motivated to do their best was paramount to his success.

## Pressing Warm Buttons

We all know how we react when a "hot button" is pressed. Unfortunately, some people take satisfaction in pressing them. They know just what to say to provoke anger. But it is just as easy to press a *warm button*. For those who never heard of such a thing, it's because while it has always been around, it has never been given a label. Let's define a *warm button* as a means of warming someone up—that is, making a person feel warm inside. It is synonymous with making someone *feel good.*

Everyone has different hot buttons, and the same is true for *warm buttons.* What provokes anger in one person may roll off the back of another. Similarly, what warms one person up may leave another feeling tepid. To address this, I developed a coaching tool called a Button Analysis. To fill it out, the coaching candidate lists everyone important to his or her work, including those at lower levels, peers, and superiors. The next step is the challenging one. Two columns are created: one for *warm buttons* and the other for hot buttons. For each individual listed, the coaching candidate is asked to identify at least one *warm button* and one hot button. Accomplishing this requires the person completing the form to observe each individual listed and ascertain what elicits warm and hot button reactions. Put another way, it requires individuals to *really* get to know the people with whom they work closely. This means observing how they relate to others and their reactions to various situations. The following is a sample of what a Button Analysis might look like:

## BUTTON ANALYSIS

| COLLEAGUES | WARM BUTTONS | HOT BUTTONS |
| --- | --- | --- |
| Boss | Pride in single-digit golf handicap | People who make excuses when a deadline is missed |
| Subordinate | Volunteer work rescuing injured birds | People who cut her off mid-sentence |

After the assignment is completed, the coaching candidate is then asked to practice pressing the *warm button(s)* of each colleague listed and make a notation of how he or she reacts. For example, to the boss who takes pride in her single-digit golf handicap, the candidate might say, "I heard how you dazzled the whole team at the company golf outing." The boss beams with satisfaction and asks if the candidate plays golf. To the subordinate who derives satisfaction rescuing injured birds: "Have you rescued any birds lately?" The subordinate responds proudly and describes the recent rescue of a Cooper's hawk. In both cases, personal connections have been made.

A problem for many is the prospect of pressing a *warm button* of someone they dislike, considering it akin to "sucking up." I recall working with a consumer-goods executive who had little respect for her boss to whom she had reported for fourteen years. Their relationship was strained, with the boss perceiving her to be self-serving because of the frequency with which she presented her case for a promotion. Upon asking her if she ever tried to make him *feel good,* she responded, "Are you kidding?" The very thought of pressing one of his *warm buttons* repulsed her. For homework, I challenged her to identify at least one *warm button* that she could press with sincerity. Two weeks later, she reported back that her boss has a collection of antique toys in his office. On her own, she complimented his collection, which prompted him to bring more in from home and share them with her. By the end of the month, her boss called me to report on her "tremendous" progress.

In the preceding example, the consumer goods executive did not grow to like her boss—but he felt she did. By showing interest in his avocation, she made him *feel good,* which in turn altered his perception of her. With a strengthening of their relationship, whether real or perceived, she was now poised to grow in her career.

What do you do when someone is difficult to read? Some people are inscrutable, presenting a pokerface rather than sharing emotions. Their offices are barren of personal effects, and they never talk about their personal lives. Such cases are challenging, but not impossible, to overcome. The techniques listed previously in the "Act as if you like someone" section would be a place to start.

For example, you could compliment a difficult person on her impressive quarterly results or on how she handled a difficult meeting. It might take time and skilled observation to identify *warm buttons,* but they exist. Everybody has them.

## Influencing: Getting Things Done Without Authority

Another interesting coaching assignment involved an information technology executive who was selected to spearhead the transformation of his company's information technology platform to meet the needs of a rapidly expanding business. While he had the technical and management expertise to serve as the project's leader, he was accustomed to getting things done by directing staff. The present challenge, however, required a leader who could work collaboratively with colleagues throughout the organization—people over whom he did not have authority. Success would depend upon his ability to build consensus around the project's goals and get key constituents committed to doing the necessary work. In other words, he had to rely heavily on his ability to *influence* his constituents.

As noted in "Managing Relationships: The Pinnacle of Emotional Intelligence," the ability to influence or persuade without direct authority is relationship management at its best. So important is this skill that businesses, governments, and volunteer organizations would not be able to survive without it. While volumes have been written on the subject, the following examples will get you on your way toward influencing effectively:

- *Credibility with your constituents.* Few would accept the leadership of someone they did not see as credible. How many times have we witnessed a politician who touts "family values" having to disqualify himself after being exposed as an adulterer? No union leader would last long if the rank and file did not view him or her as credible.

- *"I feel your pain."* Nothing brings people closer than connecting through empathy. President Bill Clinton demonstrated this brilliantly by genuinely bonding with his constituents and winning votes. On a less emotional level, getting others to buy into your ideas can be achieved more easily by demonstrating that you understand their perspective.

- *"We're all in this together."* In trying to convince others to jump onboard with your ideas, you better be prepared to answer the question "What's in it for me?" The importance of conveying "We're all in this together" cannot be underestimated. In the opening case study, the information technology executive had to convince his colleagues that a new platform would better serve *their* needs. Importantly, he had to quash any perception that they were being asked to help him advance his own agenda.

- *Resist anger when met with resistance.* It is inevitable that new ideas will be met with resistance. Some might even try to press your hot buttons. By taking the bait, a heated argument might ensue, making it all the more difficult to bring others around to your viewpoint. It is therefore crucial to remain composed and rational. This is an ideal time to acknowledge your understanding of another's feelings and his or her differing viewpoint.

- *Listen, understand, then respond.* Picking up on the last point, it is amazing how many people think that the way to bring others to their point of view is to bombard them with irrefutable information. This may work in politics with gullible voters but it seldom works in business. To the contrary, influencing people requires one to carefully listen to objections and others' viewpoints and make it known that you understand where they are coming from. Your response can then be tailored appropriately.

- *To compromise or not to compromise?* We all know the importance of give and take. What's important is to avoid giving in or taking away. For compromise to be effective, it must lead to solutions that in the long run benefit the majority. Too often, a compromise is struck that dilutes the end result to the point of rendering it ineffectual. Worse yet, the so-called leader is overly accommodating, thereby betraying those already onboard.

- *Know when it's time to leverage your boss's help.* When compromise is not warranted and you are up against a "brick wall," it may be time to leverage real power—that is, the help of your boss. This should be a last resort, since cooperation is best forged when voluntary, not forced. Nevertheless, it is a useful tool when all else fails.

- *Persevere in the face of resistance.* At times, it may feel as if you are facing a losing battle. Your colleagues have banded together to oppose you, and your boss has decided to stay out of the fray and let you handle the situation. Now is the time to re-energize your efforts and come up with a different strategy. For example, you might be able to find one person who will back you and, in turn, work behind the scenes to help you influence the others. Whatever your strategy, success in the end will require you to stay in the game.

# CHAPTER 4

# Managing the Boss

## Managing Up: You and the Boss

Being a star performer does not guarantee career success. Often, it is how well you manage the relationship with your boss that can make or break your future in a company. A case in point: A talented finance executive who made a lot of money for his company was denied a promotion after four years in the role. Instead, he was given a sizable bonus. The managing director to whom he would have reported told me privately that the executive was irritating and that she did not want him reporting directly to her. In particular, she described him as a "dog with a bone," not knowing when to back down from making his case. As such, she found herself trying to avoid him. With his career stagnated, he resigned for a comparable position elsewhere. Both he and the company lost out.

As illustrated in the previous example, managing up effectively takes more than doing your job well. We all know the importance of helping your boss to "look good," such as by ensuring that he or she is prepared for an important meeting. Equally important is to make the boss *feel good* with you around. So important is the *feel good* factor that top officials in government and business often surround themselves with longtime associates, even though they may lack requisite qualifications.

Making your boss *feel good* is not simply a matter of showering him or her with flattery. Rather, it entails building a relationship in which the boss is comfortable in your presence and assured that you are looking out for his or her best interest. Following are some tips for managing up toward that result:

- **Pick your battles carefully.** With your boss's time being valuable, you need to separate important from more routine issues, recognizing which to fight for. Also, as illustrated in the opening example, it is important to know when to back off and rest your case.

- **Keep your boss in the loop.** No one wants to be caught off guard. It is therefore wise to give your boss advance notice of a potential problem area. If you feel it necessary to go over your boss's head, make your intentions clear. Keeping your boss informed demonstrates loyalty and respect.

- **Consider how your boss thinks and processes information.** A woman I coached who was spontaneous by nature reported to a controlled and reflective boss. Not surprisingly, he was annoyed when she approached him on the spot to obtain permission to act on her ideas. The relationship improved dramatically when she put her ideas in writing, thereby giving him time to think things through.

- **Share deserved praise with your boss.** The obvious way to make your boss *feel good* is through praise. This becomes particularly challenging when you dislike your boss. For example, although your boss may take credit for your ideas, perhaps you are empowered to make decisions. You could therefore let the boss know that you appreciate that aspect of his or her management style. Sharing deserved praise is synonymous with pressing a *warm button.*

- **Ask for advice.** Asking for advice conveys your appreciation for what the boss has to offer, and also presses a *warm button.*

- **Carefully manage relationships with your boss's allies.** One needs to consider the consequences before alienating those close to the boss. A banking executive had little tolerance for an arrogant peer and frequently battled with her, even though it was known that she was the boss's protégé. Within a year, the executive's job "disappeared," and he was assigned to a lesser role. It was later learned that his peer had engineered the demotion.

- **Be discrete in voicing negative feelings about your boss to others.** You never know who might leak your confidential comments or when your negative views might be overheard and made public.

## Coping with a Difficult Boss (Part 1)

Are those close to you tired of hearing you complain about your boss? Do you dream of getting even? Unless your boss leaves, or you are fortunate enough to get a new job, you will need to learn how to cope in order to survive. In "Managing Up: You and the Boss," the focus was on general guidelines for relating effectively with your boss. This section and the next zeros in on different types of difficult bosses and suggests coping strategies.

*The bullying and intimidating boss.*

This is the proverbial "boss from hell" who derives pleasure in humiliating staff, especially in public. Often, such bosses are insecure individuals, using intimidation to ward off challenges from others. As bullies, they focus their abuse on those perceived to be weak—that is, those who will cower rather than stand up for themselves.

*Coping strategy.* Those with a thick skin who are unaffected by insults are most likely to survive. Regardless of your tolerance for verbal abuse, you need to convey your respect for the boss, but self-respect is important as well. Make it clear that you value constructive feedback but want to be treated respectfully. If the boss continues to tear you down, you might try saying, "I value your feedback but do not like being spoken to in a demeaning manner. Perhaps we can continue this conversation at a later time."

*The boss who does not support staff and allows problems to escalate.*

An insurance manager had a crucial job opening that went unfilled for six months, ostensibly because the boss would not press the case with senior management. As a result, the workload backed up and morale suffered. Such a boss can be a serious problem when it interferes with your ability to succeed.

*Coping strategy.* First, you need to ascertain why your boss has not supported you. Perhaps he or she is not committed to your request. You also need to present your case in writing, highlighting the benefits and consequences if not met. If necessary, you should suggest a joint meeting with your boss's boss.

*The boss who adds little value.*

Some may wonder why their boss was ever hired. He or she knows less than you and often gives ill-advised directives. While team building with executives in a consumer goods company, each had similar complaints regarding a newly hired senior executive whom they described as a "jerk." Morale rapidly decreased, two executives resigned for better opportunities elsewhere, and others circumvented the boss whenever possible.

*Coping strategy.* First, you need to accept reality. Unless the boss slips up, you are stuck. Circumventing your boss entails risk: He or she might have pertinent information about a particular matter or resent your actions. If you go the "Don't ask permission; ask forgiveness" route, explain why you did it—that is, why you felt it necessary to move quickly, with the company's best interest in mind. Be sure to document ill-advised directives, delineating your concerns in writing. If necessary, request a joint meeting with your boss's superior.

### The boss who adds value but is rarely available.

Such a boss is okay for those who are able to work autonomously, but an absentee boss can be stressful to those who need a sounding board and approval to proceed with their ideas.

*Coping strategy.* The key is to get on the boss's calendar, which can be done through his or her administrative assistant. Or try e-mailing your boss when you have concerns or questions.

To summarize, general guidelines for dealing with a difficult boss include the following:

- Calmly communicate your feelings and concerns, making certain that your boss is aware of what bothers you.

- Be respectful, but demonstrate self-respect as well. Expect to be treated decently and accept nothing less.

- Protect your reputation by documenting problems in writing.

If necessary, use other resources—such as a representative from human resources or senior management—to help address the problem.

## Coping with a Difficult Boss (Part 2)

The previous section focused on how to cope with different types of difficult bosses. This section expands upon that list.

### The boss who micromanages.

It is very frustrating to work for someone who tells you what to do every step of the way. He or she manages at the detail level, allowing little latitude in how you do your job. Such bosses stifle creativity and initiative. While their behavior may reflect distrust in others' judgment, it is often the case that they are well intended but hampered by perfectionism and a compelling need to avoid mistakes.

*Coping strategy.* Respectfully tell your boss how his or her management style makes you feel. Convey in a calm and reasoned manner that managing closely makes you feel mistrusted in being able to do your job without close scrutiny. It is important, though, to demonstrate that you are competent enough to be empowered.

### The taxing boss who creates unnecessary work.

This type of boss is related to the preceding type in terms of perfectionism. Such a boss goes overboard in directing staff to examine every angle of a problem before making a decision. The result is a burdening workload that often leads to unnecessary stress.

*Coping strategy.* Make a list of your deadlines and ask your boss to help you set priorities, emphasizing that the extra work will prevent you from meeting these deadlines. If possible, try reasoning with your boss, pointing out how further efforts are not apt to lead to an appreciable payoff.

### The ethically challenged boss.

The Enron fiasco and recent Bernard Madoff swindle exemplify unethical management conduct. But not all unprincipled behavior is of such magnitude. With increased pressure to squeeze out as much profit as possible, some bosses are inclined to reinterpret right from wrong. So what do you do when your boss directs you to do something that is unethical, particularly when you perceive your job to be at stake?

*Coping strategy.* There is a fine line between being a victim and participating in unethical behavior. Once you follow an unethical directive, you are a party to it. Experts recommend that you raise your concerns with your boss in a nonaccusatory manner. Put in writing your understanding of the discussion. If your boss does not back off, you are advised to go above him or her, even going so far as to the board of directors as a last resort. In most cases, internal whistle-blowers are protected legally from retaliation.

### The boss who solicits and ignores staff's ideas.

A common complaint that I hear is "There's no point in sharing my views—he just pays lip service." A case in point: The president of a company hired a chief operating officer, although serious concerns were raised by senior staff who interviewed him. I too, who conducted a pre-hire assessment, expressed concerns. In dismissing the concerns, the CEO indicated, "I had a good feeling about Joe during a round of golf." Despite the male bonding, Joe was fired a year later after alienating almost everyone with whom he worked.

***Coping strategy.*** Such a boss does not like being second-guessed, particularly when he or she feels strongly about something. The best approach is to make your case in a compelling manner, followed up in writing to protect yourself. In the end, your boss will be held accountable.

While working for a difficult boss can be challenging, it does not have to dominate your working life. Some general guidelines to help you cope include the following:

- Calmly communicate your feelings and concerns, tempering strong emotions so that your boss listens rather than becomes defensive.

- Convey respect for your boss, but also for yourself. Expect to be treated decently.

- Document problems and concerns in writing to protect your reputation.

- Recognize when to seek help from others, such as senior management, human resources, and legal counsel.

Remember, while you should not expect to change your boss, you can look out for your best interests and make the relationship more tolerable. In the end, you will have more positive energy to channel.

# CHAPTER 5

# When It's Necessary to Confront

## Healthy Confrontation in the Workplace

The word *confrontation* evokes images of hostility and combat. We all know people who angrily challenge anyone whom they perceive to get in their way. At the opposite end of the continuum are those who are non-confrontational by nature, who sweep problems under the rug in the hope that they will go away. Somewhere in the middle is the notion of *healthy confrontation.* Simply put, healthy confrontation enables an individual to tackle problems in a forthright manner that encourages resolution and minimizes a defensive and hostile response.

The importance of confrontation in the workplace cannot be underestimated. Take, for example, the following scenarios:

- A subordinate on your staff is not pulling his weight, which in turn is hurting the team's performance.

- Your boss has just given you a big project and set an unrealistic deadline.

- A surgical nurse in the operating room notices a clamp remaining in the patient's abdomen, just as the surgeon is about to suture the patient.

In each of these scenarios, an important problem needs to be addressed. How the problem is confronted will determine the outcome.

Before talking about healthy confrontation, it would be useful to talk about the extremes at either end of the continuum.

*Highly confrontational individuals* have no compunction about letting others know when they are displeased or how they feel about a matter. They tend to form quick judgments about people, jump to conclusions, and bring up problems in a way that makes others defensive. Deliberately or otherwise, they push hot buttons. The discourse in which they engage becomes highly charged versus rational, with resolution out of grasp.

*Nonconfrontational individuals,* on the other hand, resist expressing displeasure. Fearing rejection, they avoid topics that might arouse anger. Such people invariably hurt themselves and risk jeopardizing others. Think of someone you know who does any of the following:

- Fails to speak up; allows preventable mistakes to be made, or accepts blame for another's mistake

- Lets problems drag on and escalate

- Takes on more than he or she can handle; is unable to decline unreasonable demands, which in turn can lead to becoming disorganized or unable to meet deadlines

- Loses out monetarily (e.g., avoids discussing a deserved bonus with the boss)

Alternatively, *healthy confrontation* facilitates problem resolution. The next time you have a need to confront someone, try practicing the following approaches:

- **Remain calm.** Take a deep breath if you sense that a hot button is about to be pushed. While difficult to do, it's important that you resist the temptation to return an insult.

- **Pay attention to your choice of words and body language** to avoid giving the perception of being hostile or intimidating.

- **Practice empathic listening.** Let the confronted individual know that you understand his or her position, although you do not agree with it.

- **Focus on the facts of the problem without being judgmental.** To the subordinate not pulling his weight say, "I'm concerned that you are not meeting your performance goals." This will lead to a more productive conversation than saying "I'm concerned about your laziness and lousy results."

- **Express your feelings, provided they are not inflammatory.** If you are upset with a colleague who convened a meeting without your knowledge, you could say, "I'm upset you held a meeting last week without inviting me." This will evoke quite a different response than "I am infuriated that you held a meeting last week behind my back."

- **Confront the problem in a timely manner.** Your concerns will have more impact if you raise them soon after the problem occurs. However, pick a time and place that are conducive to a productive conversation.

- **Be respectful but direct** when confronting a superior or authority figure in a crisis situation. The surgical nurse in the preceding example needs to immediately and clearly inform the surgeon of the remaining clamp. Taking an oblique approach, such as "Oops, I think we forgot something," could result in a tragic mistake.

Whenever possible, confront in private. Your intention is to make your point without embarrassing the individual, which in turn might provoke a defensive or hostile response.

## Avoiding Unnecessary Confrontation:
## Four Simple Words

Several years ago, I was invited to attend an awards cere-mony for a senior executive of a national nonprofit organization. Seated next to me at dinner was the chair-man of the board. Others at the table included staff with whom I had worked throughout the years. During the main course, the chairperson lured me into a discussion about the president of the United States. After making some provocative comments, he asked for my thoughts as an observer of human behavior. Disagreeing with his observations, I candidly made my views known. He responded heatedly, and by dessert we were engaged in an uncomfortable debate. It was then that I received a folded piece of paper that was passed around the table from an individual whom I had recently coached. Upon reading it, I realized that I had forgotten the four simple words that I coach people to say when faced with a needless argument that can jeopardize an important relationship. Soon after, the chairperson made another point with which I disagreed. This time however, I looked at him squarely in the eyes and responded, *"You may be right."* With a satisfied look on his face, he indi-cated how pleased he was to win the debate.

In the previous section, "Healthy Confrontation in the Workplace," the notion of healthy confrontation as a means of resolving problem areas is examined. It is important, however, that there needs to be a problem worth standing up to, such as a colleague taking credit for your work and thereby jeopardizing your deserved bonus. At times, however, such as in the opening scenario, a confrontation of any kind should be avoided. For example, when provoked to engage in a heated discussion or argument about differing opinions, ask yourself, "Is a confrontation worth it? What is the benefit to me if I win?" The next question to ask is, "What might a confrontation cost me?" In many cases, the only real benefit is a feeling of self-satisfaction. The downside, however, might be a strained relationship with someone important to you, diminished credibility (if you lose), or getting needlessly stressed by arguing about something inconsequential. In short, diffusing a potentially contentious interaction will serve your self-interest.

Let's now look at circumstances when it is appropriate to say *"You may be right."* In general, you can use the phrase for any emotionally charged issue that it is best to avoid. Examples include such topics as these:

- Religion

- Politics

- The economy

- Social values such as those involving conservative versus liberal viewpoints (e.g., abortion rights)

Sometimes you should avoid participating in a conversation that involves bad-mouthing someone (e.g., your boss or a colleague with whom you work closely). In such cases, you need to be careful that using *"You may be right"* is not construed as agreement. An effective variation that you can use is "I haven't considered it, but you've given me something to think about."

It is very important to ensure that when using *"You may be right,"* or a variation of this phrase, your tone of voice is nondefensive, nonaggressive, and not sarcastic in the least.

For many, backing off from a confrontation can be difficult, particularly for those who hold strong opinions and have a compelling need to make their views heard. We all know people who never walk away from an argument that they feel strongly about or allow the other party to feel victorious. In the long run, however, the person who is savvy enough to avoid an unnecessary confrontation will be the winner.

# CHAPTER 6

# Thinking Smartly

## So You Think You Can Think?
## Think Again

When was the last time you gave any thought to how you think? Most of us rarely do, even though it is a key determinant of our behavior and daily decisions. Invariably, it is flawed thinking that leads to hiring or marrying the wrong person, manufacturing ill-conceived products, electing poorly qualified politicians—and the list goes on.

The good news is that all of us, regardless of innate brainpower, can improve how we think. This takes on special importance in an age when we are bombarded with information, distorted and otherwise, that aims to influence us (e.g., voting, purchasing). This section examines important principles of sound thinking that can be applied to our everyday lives at work and elsewhere.

- **The basis of sound thinking is common sense.** By definition, common sense is *sound and prudent judgment based on a simple perception of the situation or facts.* Those lacking common sense often display what is referred to as unthinking behavior. A workman removed outdoor furniture and planters from a patio to sweep it, placing the soil-laden planters on top of newly upholstered cushions. His actions were automatic and lacked common sense. An example of using common sense to the point of absurdity was a news story reporting the discovery of a dismembered body in a kitchen freezer. The police chief was quoted as saying, "We've ruled out suicide and suspect foul play."

- **Pay attention to important details.** Serious blunders can result when we make assumptions and overlook important details. During its popularity in the United States, the Chevrolet Nova was marketed in a South American country. After disappointing sales, research revealed that *No va* in Spanish means "No go." Basic research into the language and culture of a foreign country should have preceded a marketing campaign.

- **Balance optimism with caution.** The optimistic person sees the "glass half full," while those more wary see a "glass half empty." Sound decisions require a balance of the two. The president of a telecommunications company was known for positive thinking. Convinced that nothing could go wrong with a proposed acquisition, he persuaded the board of directors to sign off on his plan. Afterward, the acquisition was deemed a costly mistake. I later learned that those on his senior management team had raised concerns, only to be dismissed as naysayers.

- **Being overly cautious can be detrimental.** An investment counselor had a history of maintaining stability and respectable earnings for his clients during down markets. Being wary by nature, however, he distrusted up markets and rarely capitalized on them.

- **Stand back and connect the dots.** One can think sequentially, focusing on one thing at a time, or look at the bigger picture and connect the dots. Doing the latter enables one to identify overall patterns. A patron on a low-cholesterol diet asked his waitress if a particular soup contained cream, noting his dietary restriction. She responded affirmatively, and he selected another. Without further questioning, he ordered what he thought would be a simple, unadorned entrée. When it arrived, he was dismayed to see that it was smothered in a heavy cream sauce. Pointing it out to the waitress, she replied defensively, "You only asked about the soup."

- **Know when to second-guess yourself.** Self-confidence and decisiveness are clearly positive qualities. At times, however, it is prudent to second-guess oneself. This should not be confused with self-doubt. Rather, it refers to reviewing the facts a second time to be certain the conclusions are correct. Doing so is particularly important when the stakes are high or when accuracy is critical.

Often, I meet with clients who characteristically make a decision and move on, never pausing to think twice. This might work out in their favor most of the time, particularly if they are highly intelligent and able to quickly process information. On some occasions, however, it could backfire. Consider, for example, a portfolio manager whose stellar reputation was marred after taking a sizable stake in a company that collapsed within the year. Had he reexamined the numbers or solicited others' views, the mistake might have been avoided.

- **Trust your intuition—to a point.** At times, trusting your gut feeling pays off. Without proof, you have a sense about a salesperson and decline making an expensive purchase. The salesperson later turns out to be a swindler. Your intuition told you that something was wrong. By definition, intuition involves a person's ability to arrive at conclusions without a formal and rational examination of the facts. Studies have shown, however, that the reliability of one's intuition depends greatly on his or her knowledge, experiences, and abilities. In the previous example, the wary buyer was skilled at reading body language. However, it is important to note that one needs to recognize when to support intuitive judgments with facts. Thus while a juror might have an intuitive sense about a defendant's innocence or guilt, justice depends on a careful weighing of the facts.

Using sound thinking takes time, but not necessarily a lot of time. Doing so will help you to make good decisions in the short term and avoid making mistakes in the long term.

## Thinking Traps

By definition, a trap is a device or trick that catches its victim unaware and then disables or leaves the victim vulnerable. In a similar vein, people often fall into *thinking traps.* Once ensnared, the individual is unable to use reason, which often results in flawed decision making.

Let's look at some of the more common traps that impair our thinking and how to avoid them.

- **Overgeneralizing.** Too often, newcomers to a job routinely apply what worked in their former company to their new employer. A case in point: A newly hired plant manager who successfully increased productivity for his former employer put comparable practices in place after several months on the job. His effort was a dismal failure, with hourly workers walking off the job. So what went wrong? The plant manager had failed to consider that his new plant was unionized whereas the old was not. He fell into the trap of thinking that what worked in the past will automatically work again.

*While one indeed learns from experience, it is important to carefully evaluate each new situation to ensure that what worked in the past is transferable.*

- **Groupthink.** Few would argue that being part of a cohesive group is a positive thing. A weakness, however, is the risk of groupthink, defined as a mode of thinking characterized by members of a tightly knit group striving for unanimity, with dissent being frowned upon. As a result, contradictory views are rarely expressed and then evaluated. Take, for example, the Bay of Pigs fiasco of 1961 during which the United States invaded Cuba with the goal of overthrowing Fidel Castro. Conceived by the close-knit CIA and approved by the collegial Joint Chiefs of Staff, the plot was an abysmal failure. A review of what went wrong revealed that the Joint Chiefs of Staff readily went along with the CIA and failed to assess the risks.

    Learning from the Bay of Pigs fiasco, President John Kennedy averted a nuclear war during the Cuban

Missile Crisis by pushing his advisors to put forth their viewpoints and recommendations for action, after which the president carefully weighed all input and determined that a Russian threat was not imminent.

*Sound group decisions can be made by encouraging all participants to articulate their opinions, especially if they differ from the prevailing viewpoint. Then an objective evaluation can be made, based on all the information.*

- **Halo effect.** It is unfortunately true that attractive people have an advantage over those less physically appealing. They are more readily liked during job interviews and often are judged as more intelligent and capable. This assumption points to the *halo effect,* a thinking bias whereby our observation of one trait (e.g., good looks) influences our perception of other traits (e.g., intelligence). Once a halo is put in place, it follows the person everywhere. This phenomenon is a boon to brand marketing. For example, an individual who is highly satisfied with his top-of-the-line car might eagerly buy a lesser model from the same manufacturer for his teenager, believing that the company makes terrific cars across the board.

  *Put assumptions aside and look for supporting evidence before coming to conclusions.*

- **Cognitive dissonance.** It is human nature to want to

reduce uneasy feelings, such as those that result from holding conflicting ideas at a given moment. Cognitive dissonance is a psychological concept that describes the feeling of discomfort that results when a person holds a belief that is contradicted by another belief. While consulting with the president of a hospital, I mentioned questionable hiring decisions made by the human resources director. The president responded angrily, noting that they "go back a long time" and that she trusted him implicitly. I was fired shortly after. Unable to reconcile her positive perception of him with the information that I offered, the president eased the dissonance by denying the unpalatable input. The human resources director was later fired after it was confirmed that he had taken kickbacks from a search firm for hiring its referrals.

*Carefully evaluate contradictory beliefs and base decisions on the more compelling evidence. Keep an open mind at all times, especially when new and contradictory information arises.*

- **Wishful thinking.** This is a variation of cognitive dissonance. The scam perpetrated by Bernard Madoff represents a tragic example of wishful thinking, with investors failing to question how they could consistently get 10 percent returns during bear markets.

  *When something appears "too good to be true," it is time to inquire.*

## Critical Thinking:
## The Basis of Sound Decision Making

Deciding on whether or not to have tomato on a sandwich does not necessitate a lot of thought, but the decision to buy a sandwich franchise is another matter entirely. One would hope that careful thinking precedes making important decisions. Yet all too often, high-stakes decisions are made on the basis of a cursory review of the facts, unexamined assumptions, faulty reasoning, emotion, and/or one's gut feeling. A case in point: While consulting with a catalog company, I learned of a costly mistake made by its marketing department. After creating a beautifully photographed catalog and sending it to its customer base, sales jumped significantly. Shortly after, however, returns poured in, thereby turning profits into a net loss. What happened is that the photographs made the merchandise appear to be of higher quality than it was. Hence, when the customer received the order, anticipation was replaced by disappointment and the goods were returned.

In the preceding example, an important decision was made on the basis of *surface thinking*: "Our customers will not be able to resist buying from our beautiful catalog." While this assumption was correct, all thinking stopped there. Absent was *critical thinking*.

Simply put, *critical thinking entails rigorous thinking and involves accurately defining a problem, separating facts from assumptions, weighing and interpreting all information, including what may seem contradictory, and then drawing valid conclusions, taking into consideration the long-range implications.* Because events are often dynamic rather than static, though, critical thinking must also include the evaluation of new information as it unfolds, which might then call for new conclusions.

A useful way to approach critical thinking is to take the following steps:[1]

- **Recognize assumptions.** Assumptions are statements that are assumed to be true in the absence of proof. By recognizing assumptions, one can then separate fact from opinion.

- **Evaluate arguments.** Arguments are assertions that are intended to persuade someone to believe or act in a certain way. Evaluating arguments is the process of analyzing such assertions objectively and accurately, suspending preconceived notions.

- **Draw conclusions.** Drawing conclusions consists of arriving at judgments that logically follow from the available evidence. At this stage, it is useful to examine the possible long-range implications of one's conclusions. For example, in the catalog company example, no consideration was given to how the customer might respond to receiving merchandise that did not live up to his or her expectations.

---

1. Based on a model for the Watson-Glaser 11 Critical Thinking Appraisal, a test of critical thinking that is published by Pearson, an international media company that publishes assessment tools.

Now let's look at another example with critical thinking in mind.

In the March 13, 2011, Business Section of the Sunday *New York Times,* a lead article described the genesis of a flawed decision made by the CEO of Starbucks. In 2008, Howard Schultz decided to re-energize the company's sales by introducing a frothy and fruity drink named Sorbetto, the main ingredients of which originated in Italy. After flying to Italy to taste the ingredients and observing the success of Pinkberry, a frozen yogurt chain, Schultz was convinced that his version of a yogurt drink would be a success. By later that year, 300 Starbucks chains were promoting the new beverage. Unfortunately, customers found it to be too sweet, and the baristas balked at having to spend ninety minutes each day cleaning their Sorbetto machine. Soon after, Sorbetto was deemed a failure. So what went wrong? As one who has been decribed as moving quickly on initiatives, it is possible, although not certain, that the CEO did not critically evaluate the efficacy of Sorbetto:

- **Recognize assumptions.** Schultz may have assumed that customers would love the product. If so, this would be an opinion. Did the CEO employ market research tools such as a focus group study or pilot test prior to full implementation?

- **Evaluate arguments.** Possibly, Schultz moved too quick - ly without obtaining sufficient input from others and therefore had limited counterarguments to evaluate.

- **Draw conclusions.** If he proceeded primarily on the basis of assumptions and did not solicit sound arguments for or against his idea, the CEO was vulnerable to drawing faulty conclusions.

Being bombarded daily with information and pressed to make decisions, some with far-reaching consequences, it is important to recognize when to slow down and think carefully. In so doing, keep the following points in mind:

- **Critical thinking requires patience and self-discipline.** This does not come naturally to those who are inclined to think and act quickly.

- **Gather as much relevant information as possible.** Look for patterns, too.

- **Pay close attention to contradictory information.** Try to determine what the contradictions might mean.

- **Evaluate information objectively.** Suspend personal opinions and previous mind-sets.

- **Consider the long-term implications of decisions.** Also explore any alternative approaches that might exist.

- **Be open to changing your mind** if warranted by new information.

## Changing Your Mind:
## Weakness or Strength?

It's common to accuse politicians who change their position on issues of flip-flopping or trying to appease special interest groups. It's also common to admire those who stick to their positions, referring to them as steadfast and courageous. Undoubtedly, these judgments can be accurate portrayals. But just as often, they can be wrong.

It is not always easy to determine when it is appropriate to change one's mind. It all depends upon the individual and situation. Under some circumstances, changing one's mind might represent strength from the standpoint of the individual's willingness to re-evaluate pertinent information. On the other hand, flip-flopping might represent a weakness if the change of mind stems from self-doubt, a desire to be accommodating, or political maneuvering. In contrast, unbending adherence to a position might be the result of rigid thinking. Or it might reflect self-confidence and conviction.

### Altering a Previous Mind-set

- The parents of a teenager agree to give the car keys to their son whom they believe drives responsibly. But before the keys are turned over, they learn that their son was seen driving while drinking beer. They renege on their agreement and deny future use of the car for an indeterminate amount of time.

- A manufacturing company makes plans to acquire a floundering competitor, convinced that it can be turned around and made profitable. Prior to completion of the acquisition, information is made available to the CEO that casts a doubt on the chain's survivability. The decision to acquire is aborted.

- I once coached an executive who was exceptionally nice—to a fault. Being overly accommodating, he tried to please everyone. As such, on numerous occasions he made correct decisions that he later altered in order to appease colleagues. In backing down, results suffered.

In the first two examples, new information justified a revised plan of action going forward. Few would argue otherwise. The third scenario is another story. In this case, the executive's need for approval led him to back down from his positions, temporarily winning over colleagues but at the expense of his business.

### Resisting a Change of Mind

In contrast, we all know people who resist changing their mind, even when presented with new and compelling evidence. So what might lead to such resistance?

- **Stubbornness and/or arrogance can be deadly.** Military history points to numerous accounts of generals who marched their troops to their death, despite receiving last-minute intelligence that could have led to altered commands and saved lives.

- **Close and move on.** A need for closure is another reason someone might resist altering a decision. Those who are very transaction oriented, for instance, focus on getting things done and moving on. They are prone to ignoring new information that might require them to slow down and revisit a decision. To illustrate: An investment broker did extensive research for a client and came up with an investment plan, a component of which targeted a growing pharmaceutical. A week later, a news report implicated the pharmaceutical in a class-action lawsuit. Although the plan was not yet executed, the broker dismissed the information and committed the funds because changing that one allocation would have meant conducting a new review to find a substitute investment. A year later, the client incurred a loss that could have been avoided.

- **Get caught in a thinking trap.** Groupthink, the halo effect, and cognitive dissonance can each lead to a closed mind. With groupthink, individuals refrain from voicing their individual viewpoint, despite new information that contradicts the group's conclusion. Those smitten by the halo effect allow one trait to influence their perception of other traits, failing to evaluate each on their own merit. With cognitive dissonance, one is unable to reconcile new information with previously held perceptions.

The ability to manage a change of mind is an important component of critical thinking and can be incorporated into our everyday lives. The next time you are confronted with the possible need to revisit a decision, consider the following:

- **Examine the consequences of changing your mind** versus not changing your mind.

- **Think about why you might want to change your mind** about a decision. For example, is the reason compelling new information, a sales pitch, threats, or pressure from a special interest group?

If feasible, you might want to use others as a sounding board. Present them with the facts and see how they respond. At the very least, it will push you to think more deeply.

# CHAPTER 7

❖

# Coping with Stressful Times

## Thinking Your Way Through Stress (Part 1)

Stress is everywhere. It's an unwelcome companion to change and pressure—good or bad. A flooded basement after a heavy rain is stressful. Hard economic times that require living on a tight budget are stressful. A broken leg is stressful. And so are such life-altering events as having a baby or getting married.

In contrast to stress, distress is always negative and accompanies losses that severely tax one's ability to cope. Examples include the death of a loved one, serious illness, divorce, job loss, and homelessness from a disaster. As with your average everyday stress, however, the effects of distress can be overcome with time. One can find another job or rebuild a home. While the loss of a loved one cannot be replaced, healing can allow one to move on.

Few places are as stressful as the workplace. Production deadlines, sales goals, cutbacks and layoffs, introduction of new technology, and working for a new boss are just a few of the stresses. The promotion you fought hard for, only to feel the stress of having to prove your competency at a higher level, is another.

At times, the stress people encounter in the workplace is just the tip of the iceberg. A burned-out executive who was understaffed and denied additional staffing was offered coaching to address outbursts of anger and difficulty getting along with colleagues. After a few meetings, he shared personal burdens that he had kept to himself. Most pressing was a child who needed corrective heart surgery. In addition, the executive's widowed mother who lived nearby had recently been diagnosed with Alzheimer's disease and required home care. On top of all that, toxic mold had been discovered in his home, making it necessary for the family to vacate for a couple of weeks while the problem was corrected. The compounded stress left the executive riddled with anxiety.

This case, while extreme, lent itself perfectly to addressing his situation through a process of rational and systematic reasoning. This in turn enabled the executive to sort out the issues and gain perspective, rather than allow his emotions to cloud the situation. He was then able to *act* constructively rather than *react* inappropriately.

So how does one think through stress? I've found four basic strategies useful in helping people gain control when problems seem overwhelming:

1. **Acknowledge that your problems are getting the best of you.** Learn to recognize the symptoms that typically accompany periods of severe stress. They can be physical (fatigue, trouble sleeping, food or substance abuse), intellectual (trouble concentrating, lowered productivity, increase in mistakes), or emotional (irritability, restlessness, depression, uncontrollable anger).

2. **Identify what is most troubling to you.** A useful psychological tool is the Mooney Problem Checklist[1], which organizes problems into broad, easy-to-identify areas such as health, financial, job related, and troublesome relationships, to name a few. While you can start with a laundry list, you need to narrow it down to those stressors that weigh on you most.

3. **Set priorities.** It is now time to set priorities. What needs to be dealt with first and what can wait? The following grid is helpful in prioritizing stressors. High on the list should be important priorities that are within your immediate control. At the bottom should be relatively unimportant problems over which you have little control.

---

1. Published by Pearson, an international media company that publishes assessment tools.

| Important/Controllable | Important/Uncontrollable |
|---|---|
| EXAMPLE:<br>Scheduling heart surgery | EXAMPLE:<br>Denied additional staff at work |
| **Unimportant/Controllable** | **Unimportant/Uncontrollable** |
| EXAMPLE:<br>Your house needs painting | EXAMPLE:<br>Rain predicted for golf outing |

In the opening case study, we determined that the number-one priority was to take care of the child's corrective heart surgery. It was also important (and controllable) for the executive to find temporary housing and get needed care for his mother. His problems at work were last on the list.

4. **Examine your options and act.** This is the most satisfying stage of the problem-solving process. At this point, solutions emerge and life becomes more controllable. In the opening example, to resolve the issues the executive was able to get a month's leave of absence to deal with his child's heart surgery without the pressure of work. While the child was recovering in the hospital, the executive and his wife temporarily moved in with his mother and found live-in home care. By the end of the month, their home was decontaminated and ready for everyone to return. After going back to work with the pressing problems behind him, the executive calmly confronted his boss

and laid out the consequences of not increasing staff. Together, with the constraints in mind, they worked out a plan for getting things done.

## Thinking Your Way Through Stress (Part 2)

In addition to the four strategies outlined in "Thinking Your Way Through Stress (Part 1)," there are other points to think about when dealing with a lot of stress:

- **Set realistic goals.** After examining your options and determining the path to take, it's important to set realistic goals. The solutions do not have to be ideal —acceptable will do. As in the opening example, the executive moving in with his mother was not ideal, but it addressed two needs: temporary housing and being close to his mother until help could be found. Also, while he was unable to get his boss's approval for additional staffing, he successfully negotiated adjusted goals and timelines.

- **Be easy on yourself.** Realistic goal setting includes your need to allow a certain reduction in personal effectiveness and productivity. Few are able to perform at peak when under a lot of stress. This is not to be confused with top performance under pressure. Take professional athletes, for example. The great ones are able to remain calm and focused under pressure, but as we have witnessed, these same athletes can unravel when facing a lot of stress in their lives. The point is that the dynamo who is worried about his child's health should not expect to operate in his typical full-steam-ahead style. Very important, and a novelty for some: accept others' help. You don't need to prove that you can do it all on your own.

- **Think about what's good in your life.** When dealing with stressful times, it's helpful to reflect on your assets. Thinking about what's good in your life helps to put things in perspective and balance the negative. This in turn can help you to view your problems with a fresh approach as well as restore the energy needed to keep going. You may even discover that one of your assets might be helpful in solving some of your problems. For example, the executive in the opening scenario had a loving and supportive wife. He used her as a sounding board, and she was instrumental in finding home care for his mother.

- **Expect some discomfort even when on top of things.** Being on top of your problems does not mean that you will automatically feel better. For example, if you break a leg and have a cast put on, your leg will itch and be extremely uncomfortable until the cast is removed in several months. You're able to endure the unpleasantness, knowing it is necessary for the leg to mend properly. Similarly, experiencing multiple stressors simultaneously can be irritating despite the knowledge that all will end up well.

While most people have at one time or another experienced the negative effects of stress, there are a lucky few with a stress-resistant personality. These fortunate few innately view change as a challenge to be overcome. It energizes them. They feel in control rather than victimized. They do not allow emotions to get the best of them and rarely worry or become rattled. Can the rest of us develop a stress-resistant personality? Inspirational speakers and coaches would have you believe so. I have my doubts and suggest that such a personality is in one's genes. So where does that leave us? Worry if you must, but you don't have to have a stress-resistant personality to learn to cope effectively with difficult situations. The typical person can do it.

So how does the typical person cope effectively with stress? The answer lies in gaining control. While you might not be able to make the stressors go away, you can change how you deal with them. Thinking logically and acting practically are steps in the right direction.

## Managing Bumps Along the Road

Your job is going great when, all of a sudden, you hit a big bump in the road. It's not a blowout, but it is unsettling to say the least; and if you don't manage it appropriately, it can veer you off your path. So what are these possible bumps, and how can you handle them?

- **You are transferred to another role.** You love your job. One Monday morning, you arrive at work and are told that you will be transferring to another department. Whatever the reason for the transfer, you are devastated. You adore the team you have been working with, the product you handle, and the overall work environment. The decision is final, so trying to build a case for staying would be futile.

- **You get a new boss.** Your boss whom you highly regard has been promoted, with another taking his or her place. Being open-minded, you give the new boss a couple of weeks to settle in before making a judgment. Afterward, you identify at least five reasons why he or she was a poor choice.

- **The promotion you expected does not come through.** You've worked hard and have been led to believe that a promotion was forthcoming. But when the time comes, you're told that it will take a little longer than expected. At first you react with disbelief, which soon turns to outright anger.

- **Your job description changes.** Just last weekend at a social gathering, you told friends how much you liked your job. Then, without warning, your job description changes, with interesting parts of your job going to someone else. In turn, increased paperwork has been added to your responsibilities.

- **You are asked to relocate.** You and your family are quite comfortable in the community in which you live. A reorganization within your company, however, results in your job being moved to another city. You are offered the opportunity to relocate. While the new city is attractive, you and/or your family have reservations.

- **Your overall compensation (base, bonus, options, commission) is cut.** You have been making either a comfortable living or one that allows you to just get by. With business in a decline, you learn that your overall compensation will be lowered.

These and equally disconcerting setbacks happen all the time, especially in a changing world. While ideal resolutions are unlikely, there are steps you can take to deal with them in a rational and productive manner.

### In general

- Refrain from saying or doing anything until you think the situation through. Take some time to process what you have been told. It is especially important that you do not react angrily and say something that you might later regret.

- Also refrain from complaining to your colleagues. Messages have a way of becoming distorted and going public. You need to control your response to the situation.

- Re-read "Thinking Your Way Through Stress."

### Adjust your mind-set

- Put the situation in perspective. All too often, we turn a bump into a catastrophe, which only makes it more difficult to deal with.

- Be introspective and reflect on your feelings and the facts of the situation. For example, are you upset that you got a new boss or angry that you were not promoted to the position? Often, realization of our true feelings helps us to better manage the stress associated with the bump.

### Take control: Empower yourself to act

- Examine if options exist. For example, there may be other job opportunities either within or outside the company. Or, if asked to relocate, perhaps you can negotiate a long-distance commute, which has become popular with couples when one cannot leave.

- Identify someone with whom you can confidentially discuss the situation and vent your feelings. An unbiased perspective might provide useful insights.

- Once you are calmed down and have had time to think things through, discuss your concerns with your boss. Perhaps there is some wiggle room for negotiation.

- Develop a plan for the long haul. While you need to deal with the immediate situation, you also need to start planning for the future. Don't put your future in the hands of the company—put it in your hands.

Bumps in the road are inevitable. The following simple principle will help you to get over them and back on track:

*Don't get mad. Don't get even.*
*Get ahead: Take control.*

❖

# CHAPTER 8

# *Projecting Your Best*

## Image Management:
## The Good, The Bad, The Ugly (Part 1)

During an assessment of a managerial candidate, nothing memorable occurred until I asked him to identify an animal that he might like to be if not himself. His response was immediate: *"What kinds of animals does the company hire?"* I had never received such a response before, and I found it clever. But after reviewing all information from the assessment, a potential liability emerged, with that response summing it up. Bent on making a favorable impression, the candidate was prone to manipulating his image. Coming across as disingenuous, such people run the risk of undermining trust. He was not hired (for other reasons), and it was later learned through contacts in the business that he was regarded as a phony who said what he thought others wanted to hear.

Image management is just what it sounds like:

managing one's image to come across in a desired way. People in all walks of life do it, as do companies and other entities. Take for example how British Petroleum (BP) responded to the Gulf oil spill, spending billions to repair the damage as well as to manage its image as a responsible corporate citizen. We all know people who present a public persona, displaying to the world how they want to be seen through their appearance, behaviors, and how they communicate. When executed properly, the results can be rewarding. Effective image management wins elections and can help to put people on a fast career track. When done poorly, it can be detrimental to one's career.

Pundits would argue that Senator Robert Dole's inability to get past his dour image contributed to the loss of his presidential bid. In another example, a talented marketing executive was passed over for a big promotion. I later learned that senior management had concerns regarding his fake-looking toupee and how it might distract key clients. In both cases, the individual's image raised questions with their target audience.

Image management is taught at an early age. It's commonplace for parents to tell their young children to be on their best behavior when out in public. By puberty, teens in need of acceptance by their peer group are obsessed with their appearance. By the time we're ready for college or a job interview, the importance of making a favorable impression is well ingrained in our psyche.

A question that often arises is whether image management is nothing more than manipulation—and therefore a bad thing. To simplify matters, let's look at image management in three ways: *the good, the bad, and the ugly.* We'll define *good* image management as a tool that furthers the goals of the doer with no harm to others. *Bad* image management involves clumsy manipulative behavior with the potential to impair the doer's image. Finally, *ugly* image management crosses the line to being deceptive and unprincipled, with the potential to harm those being manipulated.

- **Good image management: The Grecian Formula approach.** The savvy individual recognizes the importance of playing to his or her audience through image management. One way is to simply look and act your best. There are many ways to accomplish this. Some minimize their grey hair to project greater vitality. Others engage a speaking coach. Politicians routinely kiss babies to show they have a sensitive side. Whether deliberate or not, the 2011 *American Idol* winner wore a cross around his neck, which may have given him an advantage with Christian voters. In each case, the doer benefited without harm to others.

- **Bad image management: Poorly executed manipulation.** I vividly recall having a meeting with the general counsel of a client company. At one point, we were interrupted by a phone call from his secretary. He put the secretary on hold and asked me to leave for a few minutes, noting that the president needed to consult with him on an urgent matter. I later learned that he routinely does this when wanting to impress someone. Similarly out to impress was a job candidate who had a lot vested in being perceived as a superior person. Accordingly, he relentlessly touted his accomplishments, deflected blame for any mistakes, and name-dropped throughout the interview. In both examples, the doer poorly executed an attempt to impress. Unless the audience is gullible, this is bad image management.

- **Ugly image management: Deceptive and damaging.** The Bernard Madoff swindle that cost many their life savings represents image management at its ugliest. By presenting himself as a savvy investment manager, Madoff successfully misled investors and financial experts alike—until caught. Anytime someone engages in self-promoting behavior at the expense of another, image management rears its ugly head. A particularly pernicious form is when an individual tries to elevate his or her own image by deceptively attacking that of another. We're all tired of vicious political campaigns that distort the truth in an attempt to damage an opponent's credibility. Two people vying for the same promotion can lead to one or both denigrating the other behind the scenes. These kinds of image management are deliberate and all too often are effective as a means to an end. But, fortunately, the perpetrators can also fall flat.

## Image Management:
## The Good, The Bad, The Ugly (Part 2)

As we have seen, image management varies in degree. At its best, it can help an individual to come across favorably with no harm to others. Done badly, it can make the doer look foolish. At its worst, image management advances the interests of one party at the expense of another.

As a personal development strategy, good image management requires a moderate to high level of emotional intelligence. Before being able to map out a plan for self-improvement, you first need to realistically see yourself as others see you. Are you able to read people with whom you interact and gauge how they react to you? For example, a hard-driving financial services manager had the habit of multitasking while meeting with staff and cutting them off if they did not quickly get to the point. Not surprisingly, they perceived her to be uninterested in them and much more task oriented than people oriented. She was totally unaware of how she came across, perceiving herself to be kindhearted and welcoming. While she was in fact, a caring individual, her outward image masked those qualities.

Let's now take a closer look at how people can assess the image they cast and bring it more in line with the image they want to project.

## Do You See What Others See?

Before leaving for work, take a look at yourself in a full-length mirror. What do you see? Are you well groomed or careless with your appearance? Are you stylish or conservative? Is your appearance age and job appropriate? A local television personality had a reputation for dressing like a seductive teenager. Being talented, however, she was lured away to another station. Her debut revealed a remarkable transformation. Most likely as a result of image coaching, she now projected sophistication and professionalism.

An effective way to ascertain how others perceive you is to ask them. I once worked with a sales manager who made a lot of money for his company but, nevertheless, was close to being fired unless he turned around his behavior. Being attention seeking, he regularly told inappropriate and "politically incorrect" jokes, leading senior management to worry that he might embarrass the company. Seeing himself in an entirely different light, it was necessary to make him aware of how others perceived him. I therefore conducted 360° interviews.[1] The bottom line was that he was seen as decent and likeable but also as a jokester with questionable social

---

1. 360° interviews represent a powerful information-gathering tool whereby a circle of people who work closely with someone are interviewed. Included are those at a lower level (such as staff), peers, and superiors. The purpose is to assess how the interviewees perceive the individual in question.

judgment. He was stunned at the feedback and highly motivated to repair his image.

In an opposite vein, others may perceive you more favorably than you do. For example, an engineer was promoted to manager of his department. He was shocked, perceiving himself to be smart but lacking in charisma and leadership skills. In reality, although shy, he was highly regarded throughout the company and one to whom people turned for advice and counsel.

### How Do You Want to Be Seen?

Hopefully, you like what you see when you look in the mirror and your self-perception is in alignment with how others see you. If there is a disconnect, however, then it may be time to adjust your image. For example, let's say that a seasoned grievance counselor who takes pride in his ability to console others is given feedback that he comes across on occasion as hard-nosed and unsympathetic. The questions he needs to ask are these: "What behaviors conveyed this?" and "What can I do to change this perception?" Perhaps the counselor asked too many questions and did not take enough time to allow the grieving person to emote. Next time, he makes it a point to listen more and encourage the individual to express his or her feelings.

### Above All Else, Be True to Yourself

Projecting the best image you can does not mean that

you should try to alter your true nature. According to some pundits, Katie Couric failed as the CBS anchor-woman because she lacked the gravitas needed for viewers to take her seriously. Should she adjust her image and try again? In this case, good image management might be for her to find a different role where her pleasing and perky qualities will be an asset.

# CHAPTER 9

❖

# *Grow on Your Own*

## Career Advancement: Is Moving Up the Only Way to Get Ahead? (Part 1)

Getting a promotion or better job elsewhere is indeed satisfying, especially when you've worked hard and are being recognized for your accomplishments. For some, however, moving up can be the wrong move. To illustrate: As part of a large bank's succession-planning efforts, I evaluated the top fifteen executives deemed to have advancement potential. The purpose was to help ensure that each candidate had the right mix of qualities to succeed at a higher level and identify strengths and weaknesses so that development plans could be put in place. After providing feedback to the candidates, five dropped out of the program, recognizing they would have been either unhappy or in over their heads. For these aspiring and talented people, how can they advance in their careers without moving up? Chapter 9 takes a look at the implications for moving up to a higher level, how to determine if a new opportunity is right for you, and, alternatively, how to grow in your present job.

Those who seek career advancement are typically ambitious and motivated by the prospect of attaining more of the following:

- **Salary and perks**—a higher standard of living for themselves and their families

- **Power or influence**—having a greater span of control and influence in decision making

- **Status and prestige**—obtaining the respect and admiration that accompanies a bigger job

- **Challenges**—the opportunity to prove competency in a more difficult role

In addition, at times an organization needs you to move up to fill an opening. Trusting that the organization knows best, you accept.

Most of the time, people make sound career choices, and with support from the organization, they transition smoothly and thrive. But while advancement provides opportunity, it can also entail risk and sacrifices. So what are some of the implications associated with advancement?

- **New learning curve.** A bigger role typically involves a learning curve and the need to prove one's credibility all over again.

- **Increased pressure and stress.** Moving up often requires working longer hours and is associated with increased pressure, particularly until one gets up the learning curve. This in turn can have a negative impact on one's personal and family life. Pressure is also associated with having to sustain a higher standard of living.

- **The possibility of getting in over your head.** The Peter Principle states that people are promoted as long as they are competent. Eventually, they reach a level at which they are incompetent—that is, they take on more than they can handle and fail. A case in point: The manager of a 250,000-square-foot tire distribution center was promoted to oversee an 800,000-square-foot facility. He was terminated a year later because the job was too complex and demanding.

- **Possible need for relocation.** Relocation often entails lifestyle changes (e.g., moving from a large East Coast city to a rural Midwest town). It can also be an issue for dual-career couples. Increasingly, one stays behind with the children while the promoted spouse "commutes" long distance, seeing the family on weekends.

- **New job specifications.** Moving up often means taking on different duties, which may not represent a "good fit" (see Chapter 2, Moving Toward the Right Career Path). A successful merchandise control analyst accepted an advancement opportunity to become a buyer, requiring him to work less with numbers and more with vendors. Being more analytical than intuitive and uncomfortable in a role that required him to schmooze and negotiate, he was unhappy as a buyer. Fortunately, he was able to return to his former role. Many in sales do not aspire to move up to sales management. They enjoy selling and prefer to work in the field with customers.

The purpose of the preceding is not to scare you off but, rather, to encourage you to "look before you leap."

## Career Advancement: Is Moving Up the Only Way to Get Ahead? (Part 2)

As discussed in "Career Advancement: Is Moving Up the Only Way to Get Ahead? (Part 1)," moving up to a bigger job is not necessarily right for everyone. While a presumably better opportunity may present itself as tempting, you must remain aware of the potential risks and pitfalls. Given the pluses and minuses, it is important to weigh the following considerations:

- **Job fit.** Is there a good fit between you and the new job responsibilities? For example, in considering a promotion from manufacturing engineer to manufacturing manager, you need to ensure that you have the right mix of abilities, operational style, personality, and interests to succeed. It is imperative for you to be fully aware of what you will be getting into and how well you will fit with the new role.

- **Corporate culture.** This is particularly relevant if you are moving to another company. Are your values and style compatible with the new company? This past year, I witnessed a talented executive lose his job after it became apparent that his aggressive style and singular focus on results did not fit the company's people-oriented culture.

- **Your prospective boss.** Is the boss someone with whom you can relate effectively? If you prefer to operate with a high degree of autonomy, will the boss allow it, or does he or she manage closely?

- **Motives for wanting the job.** To what extent will the opportunity satisfy your motivation(s) for wanting the job (e.g., more money and perks, greater power)?

- **Impact on your personal/family life.** How will the bigger job impact your personal and family life? Will you need to work longer hours? Relocate? Consideration must be given to everyone concerned, and their participation in the decision making can help avoid strife down the road.

- **Employer's expectations.** In accepting a new job, it is crucial to clearly understand what will be expected of you at critical milestones, such as in six months and a year later. Are the expectations realistic and can you meet them?

Let's say you have decided that moving up is not for you or advancement opportunities are limited. Assuming you are motivated to develop further, there are steps you can take to grow within your present job. See if any of the following appeal to you:

- **Take on bigger challenges.** Seek opportunities that represent a learning experience. One builder declined a project that involved adding an octagon-shaped addition to a home, noting that he could make more money building "boxes." Another builder was eager to stretch himself for the job, which in the long run helped him to take on a greater variety of projects.

- **Improve productivity and profitability.** Perhaps you can work smarter and find ways to operate more efficiently and improve productivity. A sales representative, for example, can try to expand his or her sales territory or target more profitable customers. A plant manager can identify ways to improve quality and reduce scrap.

- **Acquire added skills and greater expertise.** If so inclined, you can consider getting a college or advanced degree or taking courses to acquire new skills and improve your expertise.

- **Mentor others.** A fifty-eight-year-old executive reached a plateau in his career. Not ready to retire and feeling disheartened, I suggested that he consider a new purpose: to focus on developing his staff, with their success being part of his legacy. Two years later, he is enjoying considerable satisfaction in having helped three staffers earn promotions.

By developing in your present role, you will not only feel good about yourself but you will be better prepared if a desirable opportunity comes along.

# *Final Thoughts*

It's springtime in New England, the busiest season for avid gardeners. I bring this up because gardening can be a metaphor for effectively managing your career. It is not enough to simply put a plant in the ground and expect it to flourish. Nor is it enough to learn the strategies presented in the preceding pages and expect your career to take off. Creating a beautiful garden takes hard work beyond planting. It requires regular fertilizing, weeding, mulching, aerating, pruning, dividing, deterring critters, and so on. Similarly, a thriving career requires ongoing attention. For example, you will need to practice the techniques presented, observe their impact, and do any necessary tweaking to obtain the desired effect.

Let's look again at the two key skill areas that are paramount to career success: the ability to think rationally and the ability to relate effectively. Staying with the gardening metaphor, it's no coincidence that we refer to the building of strong working relationships as "cultivating relationships." It takes time, skill, and practice to accomplish this. An example that comes to mind involved a coaching engagement with an executive who experienced difficulty in the interpersonal arena. During a session with him, he described a failed attempt to make an overweight co-worker *feel good*. He added that his job required him to collaborate with her on a daily basis. With the *feel good factor* in mind, he told her one day, "Nice outfit—slims you down." She apparently did not take kindly to his remark and walked off in a huff. After we discussed the incident, he soon realized that his "compliment" was interpreted as "I like your outfit. It makes you look less fat." The point is that, for some, skillful application of the strategies presented will require practice, tweaking, and more practice.

Thinking effectively also takes practice, particularly since flawed thinking patterns tend to be deeply ingrained. Again, the gardening metaphor applies. Thus we refer to critical thinking as "digging beneath the surface" and the development of new ideas as "groundbreaking." Those who tend to make quick decisions primarily on the basis of their intuition will indeed have a tough time slowing down and digging for facts to support their decisions. Knowing what they need to do to ensure sound decision making is one thing. Practicing it successfully and making it a habit constitute another.

Your journey toward a more satisfying career does not have to be taken alone. When feeling lost, seek out a trusted colleague, friend, or family member to be a sounding board. Perhaps someone at work could serve as your mentor. You might also want to consider engaging a coach to help along the way. In the long run, however, you—not your employer or trusted others—need to steer your own career. Take charge and thrive!

# About the Author

**Danella Schiffer, Ph.D.**, is an industrial/organizational psychologist. She has devoted her career to helping individuals reach their career potential while ensuring that organizations hire the most qualified, develop the most promising, and improve organizational effectiveness so that all can contribute to meeting business goals.

Throughout her extensive career, she has worked with hundreds of individuals ranging from entry-level staff to chief executive officers in diverse organizational settings. Trained in both industrial and clinical psychology, Dr. Schiffer understands the relationship between individual and organizational effectiveness. Her insightfulness about people, combined with a pragmatic and bottom-line orientation, have enabled her to work successfully with differing individual styles.

In addition to business consulting, Dr. Schiffer works privately with individuals. She has published numerous articles on career issues and has been quoted in the *New York Times, Wall Street Journal,* and popular magazines. Dr. Schiffer obtained her Ph.D. in Industrial/Organizational Psychology from New York University, is licensed to practice in Connecticut and New York, and is a member of the American Psychological Association.